Goodbye,

faithful
friend

Remembering your Dog with Love

by
Marianne Richmond

Goodbye, faithful friend

© 2005 by Marianne Richmond Studios, Inc.

Marianne Richmond Studios, Inc.
420 N. 5th Street, Suite 840
Minneapolis, MN 55401
www.mariannerichmond.com

ISBN 0-9770000-1-X

Illustrations by Marianne Richmond

Book design by Sara Dare Biscan

Printed in China

First Printing

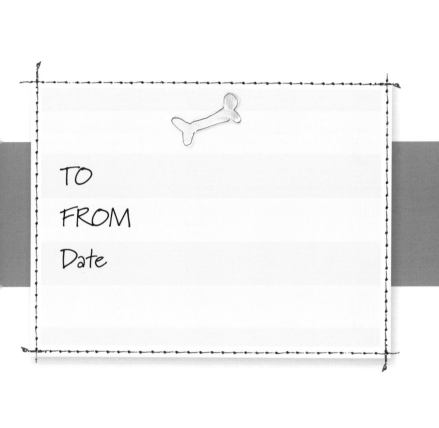

TO

FROM

Date

I know your
heart is broken
over the loss
of your faithful
friend.

I wanted you
to know
I'm thinking
about you
during this
sad time.

Some people might not recognize
the depth of your grief.

Perhaps you weren't sure how
you'd react... and your
emotions surprise you.

I understand your dog was a
wonderful part of your family,

and the pain of
this loss is
real and profound.

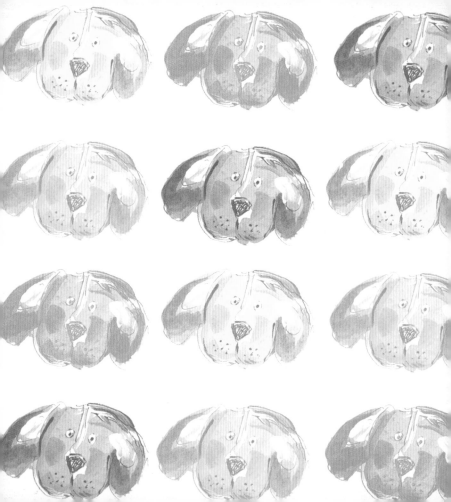

I imagine you have in your
mind a hundred things
you'll miss about that
sweet dog of yours...

The way he'd eagerly greet you,
like it had been years since
you two had seen each other

(instead of the 30 seconds
it had been)!

The way he was always up for a game of fetch or a walk around the neighborhood.

His endearing quirks, unpredictable fears and charming "dog traits."

And, of course, his unconditional love that melted your heart.

Thank goodness
   for memories.
For as long as
   memories live
within your heart,
   your gentle,
noble friend will
   live forever.

I would guess that certain times of day will be harder than others... moments when your dog was just "there."

You'll miss the jingle of his collar, the comfort of his footsteps or the sound of his bark.

And, of course, the
spirited wag of his tail.

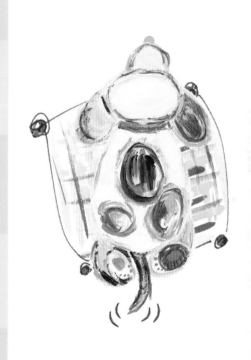

There will never be another dog like yours. Nor would you want there to be. He was one-of-a-kind — your faithful friend.

Perhaps someday you will welcome another dog into your home. But, for now, may you feel fortunate to have known the special bond between smitten owner and beloved pet.

Losing a best animal friend is truly

one of life's toughest experiences.

Remember your
dog with love...

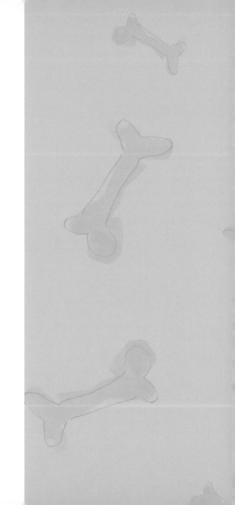

as we will, too.

We care about you
in your sadness...

and send you
our heartfelt
sympathy.

A gifted author and artist, Marianne Richmond shares
her creations with millions of people worldwide
through her delightful books, cards, and giftware.
In addition to the *Simply Said...* and *Smartly Said...*
gift book series, she has written and illustrated five
additional books: **The Gift of an Angel,
The Gift of a Memory, Hooray for You!,
The Gifts of Being Grand** and **I Love You So....**

To learn more about Marianne's products, please visit
www.mariannerichmond.com.